ABCs of A Nobody

Jake Raymund Aringay

BookLeaf
Publishing

Presentation by *BookLeaf Publishing*

Web: www.bookleafpub.com

E-mail: info@bookleafpub.com

ISBN: 978-93-95784-36-8

First edition 2022

DEDICATION

This book is dedicated to all the nobodies out there. I feel you, and you are not alone.

ACKNOWLEDGEMENT

While the journey to this point was not easy, I have lived to see the day my poetry collection is published. All of this is not possible without the help and support of my family, relatives, friends, and close friends.

To my parents, I am forever in debt to you for having raised and supported me in my entire life, even during my ups and downs. I am eternally grateful to my sisters and their families for welcoming, supporting, and taking care of me while I am staying in Australia. To my youngest brother, I am deeply thankful to you for constantly trying to make me laugh with memes and hilarious videos.

To my sworn friends – Kert and Adz. Thank you for everything. There are too many to mention, but the most important thing I wanted to thank you for being there unconditionally and giving me a space to confide in everything. I appreciate your patience in putting up with my antics, and I hope you will continue to put up with them for a long time.

To my brothers in The Gud Companie, BJ, and Raz, I am grateful for the friendship and your unwavering support in so many things – technical challenges, feedback for pitching, writing ideas, and especially being a good company. I am looking forward to reviving our podcast project in the future.

To my closest university classmates, Bowie, Luis, and Rahul, I am deeply thankful for your friendship and support while I attended university. All this time, I thought I'd be alone in my studies. It turned out that I'd spend my three years with you being my best mates in Australia.

Finally, to all those who have been a part of my writing journey: Xericho, Mark Andre, John Marvic, Errol, Verona, Kyle, Johndale, Ella, and Alyssa

PREFACE

This book contains 21 poem creations crafted to accomplish the #TheWriteAngle writing challenge. The general theme these creations follow is the letters of the alphabet, with the only exception that five letters are not included given the number constraint.

The creations in this book are inspired by various excerpts and experiences of my personal life in poetry form. I would always like to think that I am not a significant person, that I am simply a nobody. Hence, this book is titled ABCs of A Nobody.

I have never published anything before, and it has always been a dream of mine to do so at least once in my lifetime. I have been in a writing slump for several years now, leaving hills of ideas untouched – that is why I wrote this collection, hoping to get back the drive to write again.

A Bittersweet Memory

A long time ago,
A certain island from that archipelago.

A summer glistened like amber,
A fateful encounter I would always remember.

Arabica was her cup of coffee,
Arabica was a beverage I would get iffy.

Arugulas, I thought, was healthy and green,
Arugulas, she expressed, were not greens she was
keen.

At certain times we would fight,
At certain times everything is alright.

At some point, our bond no longer held well,
At some point, it was finally time to say farewell.

Autumn dyed the meadows red,
Autumn died as soon as the winter tears were shed.

All these times made us happy and weary,
All of which ended only becoming a bittersweet
memory.

But Sometimes

Books are meant to be opened and read,
But sometimes they are our own pages that are
left unread.

Buttons are meant for the curious to be pressed,
But sometimes they are seemingly better left at
rest.

Bridges are meant to be crossed,
But sometimes we are too afraid we leave it
uncrossed.

Balloons are meant to fly in the sky,
But sometimes we hold it back from going up
too high.

Bottles are meant to hold liquid of finite
capacity,
But sometimes we fill it beyond overflowing
insanity.

Battles are meant to be fought and won over,
But sometimes losing them makes us think it is
over.

Barbarians are meant to be masters in facing any
difficulty or distress,
But sometimes they have thoughts they can't
express.

Boxes are meant to contain various things and
objects,
But sometimes the items are random just like
this poem's contents.

Connecting with Someone

Connecting with someone takes more than just a
link between us and them.
Connecting with someone takes more than just
us vibing in our realm.

Checking on someone takes more than just
messages we have sent.
Checking on someone takes more than just the
call times we have spent.

Caring for someone takes more than just us
saying that we care.
Caring for someone takes more than just us
showing that we're there.

Cheering up someone takes more than just us
telling them it's okay.
Cheering up someone takes more than just us
hearing the burdens they weigh.

Crushing on someone may take more than just
an infatuation.
Crushing on someone may be a result of a
wishful imagination.

Confessing your love for someone may take a
lot of courage and determination.
Confessing your love for someone may end up
in rejection and frustration.

Courting that someone may be a result of a
successful confession.
Courting that someone may end up in a
relationship worth a celebration.

Continuing life with your new significant other
is a wonderful feeling.
Continuing life with them adds to the world new
meaning.

Dear Friend

Dear friend,
Days have passed without me missing you to no
end.

Dashing gracefully, I remember.
Denying your skill, I felt your temper.
Devoting time for your craft with no signs of
surrender.

Dear friend,
Days without your presence are difficult to
pretend.

Demanding eccentrically, I look back.
Demonstrating your dominance, I was taken
aback.
Defying logic against others you would strike
back.

Dear friend,
Days I have spent with you, I wish I could
extend.

Departing suddenly, I amassed regrets.
Daydreaming, I would hear your voice, but all I
see are silhouettes.
Disappearing from my life, just like how the sun
sets.

Elusive Lady

Elusive lady for days,
Enclose me in your arms' warm embrace.

Elated by your sudden appearance, I was
excited.
Exalted as you beamed rays of light, the sun
slowly subsided.
Enthused by your beauty and glamour, people
flocked and gathered.

Elusive lady of the night,
Entice me a song of delight.

Enchanted by your presence, I was mesmerized.
Exposed by moonlight, gems sparkled like your
tender eyes.
Endowed with a mysterious power, rendering
anyone paralysed.

Elusive lady at daybreak,
Extinguish me from my sorrows by the great
lake.

Encompassed by your afterimages, I felt
surrounded.
Engrossed by the auroras it emitted, the place
expanded.
Enamoured by your smile, leaving hearts
glistened.

Family

Families are a joy, if not, one of the most
incredible things in the world.
For us children, we are provided food, clothing,
and shelter by our parents.
For parents, being healthy and seeing our
brightest smiles bring happiness.

Families do not always have to follow
conventional composition.
For some, they only have a mother or a father,
not both.
For others, they have two mothers or two
fathers.

Families do not always have to be blood-related.
For some, they are grateful to be taken care of in
orphanages.
For others, they are fortunate to be chosen and
loved by adoptive parents.

Families are not always about good and happy times.
For some days, we live through storms and disasters.
For other days, we experience a roller coaster of emotions.

Families, we pray, will always be there for each other.
Families, we pray, will unconditionally love one another.
Families, we pray, will always be on our journey together.

Given A Chance

Gone are the days when our cries are easily
appeased.
Gone are the days when making faces no longer
made us wheeze.
Gone are the days when we stopped looking
forward to surprises being teased.

Going back, we enjoyed those simpler times.
Going back, we played with grimes and slimes.
Going back, we listened to songs filled with
rhymes.

Gone are the days when we could freely make
mistakes.
Gone are the days when our failures can be
mended by retakes.
Gone are the days when we dashed through life
without stepping on the brakes.

Going back, we stood up every time we fell.
Going back, we learned as fast as cars would
accel.
Going back, we persevered through hardships
even if we were unwell.

Given the option, I would revisit the past.
Given the opportunity, I would tell my old self
the world is vast.
Given a chance, memories from back then
would always last.

Happiness

Happiness.

Its definition can be found in various sources of knowledge.
However, when asked the question, it can prove difficult to answer.

What is happiness?

Straightforward as it is, the time it takes to respond differs from one to another.
They say the longer it takes to find an answer, the less likely they can.

Happiness?

Some may take the easy route and look up a dictionary to find the definition.
A few could take minutes to several hours to compose their thoughts and respond.

What is happiness?

Even when given the time to sort out what is in
their mind,
They still are searching for the answer they are
meaning to find.

Happiness.

Kudos to those who have taken years of pursuit
to finally get their answer.
Respect for everyone else who has taken a
lifetime yet still could not find theirs.

Imagination

Imagination – was vast and deep at the time.
It was one thing I was very abundant in.
It was one thing that kept me alive and sane.
It was, what I think, was my sole purpose of living.

Imagination – was so strong and intense.
It was at one point in time that I could no longer handle it.
It was gradually leaking out of the shell I tried containing it in.
It was futile, as I left myself with an almost empty vessel.

Imagination – every little bit of it left I tried grasping.
It was a struggle until I acknowledged it was pointless.
It was a tragedy so bad that I started denying it.
It was hopeless – this was the reality I accepted.

Imagination – a tiny speck of it seems nothing.
It was a gamble of risk and uncertainty.
It was a battle I had nothing to lose.
It was slowly filling up as if telling me not to give up.

Jacarandas, Jacarandas, Jacarandas

Jacarandas have a special place in my heart.
Just as vibrant as they were when I first
encountered it.
Jubilant are my thoughts now when I see one.

Jacarandas start off like any other flower trees.
Just spreading lush green leaves on its branches.
Jocund as the shade it provides breezes cool
fresh air.

Jacarandas in full bloom is a sky filled with
lavender.
Just standing in its presence, you are awed into
silence.
Jittery as I am, its marvellous shine brings
calmness.

Jacarandas, Jacarandas, Jacarandas.
Just when I thought I would never see them
again.
Jumping in joy when its flowers start dropping
into my head.

Kindred Spirits

Kaleidoscopic. Monochromatic.
Knowledgeable. Gullible.
Kind-hearted. Hard-hearted.

Kindred bodies separated.
Kindred souls liberated.
Kindred beings never faded.
Kindred spirits gathered.

Kind-hearted. Hard-hearted.
Knowledgeable. Gullible.
Kaleidoscopic. Monochromatic.

Love, Love, Love

Love can be described through a multitude of
words.
Love can be shown through a myriad of actions.

Love can be superficial.
Love can be profound.
Love can be motivational.
Love can be unconditional.

Love can be given.
Love can be taken.
Love can be accepted.
Love can be rejected.

Love can be observed.
Love can be ignored.
Love can be expressed.
Love can be suppressed.

Love, Love, Love.
Love, even after life, will still be love.

Memories, Melodies, and Melancholies

Memories of the past shaped who we are in the present.
Memories of the present will determine who we will be in the future.

Melodies of the past mold the music we are enjoying in the present.
Melodies of the present will serve as the music our next generations will enjoy in the future.

Melancholies of the past paved way to changes we thought we would never get in the present.
Melancholies of the present will become inspirations for changes we will achieve in the future.

Nostalgia's Adventure

Nostalgia once met the present.
Navigated through its memories that were
pleasant.
Noticed it was very fond of them.
Nit-picked through each one to find the best
gem.

Nostalgia took this treasure.
Nibbled around it on leisure.
Naïvely thought of bringing it back.
Not knowing it wouldn't fix the crack.

Nostalgia tried its best.
Nonchalantly brought back things that were
reminiscent.
Normally remnants have passed.
Not as nostalgic as they were in the past.

Oh Olivia

Oh Olivia

Oh, Olivia, nice to meet you!
Recalling the first time my eyes gazed upon you.
You looked so tiny I thought my hands were too
big to hold you.

Oh, Olivia, our sweet angel.
Recalling the first time my arms lifted and
carried you.
You felt so small I thought my large body was
too big to contain you.

Oh, Olivia, our cheerful young lady!
Recalling the first time my ears heard your
talking voice.
You sounded like a charmer I thought my face
couldn't stop smiling in rejoice.

Oh, Olivia, our little diva!
We await your lovely songs and graceful dances.
We look forward to your little adventures in life.

Raphael Gene

Raphael Gene, we welcome you to this world.
Ah, in those little eyes were everyone's different
expressions of joy.
From your tiny mouth, we heard breathing,
burping, and crying sounds.
Flapping your baby arms, you would
instinctively reach out to ours.
Your well-being was our top priority.

Raphael Gene, a year has passed by quickly.
Ah, coming from your tiny lips were the first
words you have spoken.
From your developing legs, we saw you
struggling to stand straight.
Flapping your little feet, you would start
learning how to walk.
Your growth was steadily progressing.

Raphael Gene, you are in your third year.
Ah, from across the hallway, I knew you were
awake.
From your playroom, you would scream your
lungs out singing.
Flailing your arms, stomping your feet, you
would be all over the house.
Your toddler journeys are something we await in
excitement.

Silence

Silence can be interpreted in different ways.
It can be bad in certain ways.
But it can also be good in some ways.

Some say it is a world devoid of sound.
Inside that world, no one would hear anything.
Inside that world, everyone is at peace with
themselves.

Some refer to it as a being that takes away
people's voices.
It serves as a punisher of the wicked.
It serves as a saviour of the oppressed.

Some treat it as the aftermath of an explosion.
The result that its victims are left weeping.
The result that its beneficiaries are left rejoicing.

Silence can still be described in other ways.
It can be good in specific ways.
But it can also be bad in some ways.

To Be A Creator

To be a writer, I aspired to be.
I wrote snippets and pieces of poetry.
I transformed my ideas into short stories.
Until I reached a wall I couldn't break.

To be a composer, I aspired to be.
I played instruments and listened to music.
I made melodies and wrote songs.
Until I reached a pitch I couldn't reach.

To be a creator, I aspired to be.
I created scenarios and built worlds.
I designed creatures and forged weapons.
Until I have reached an enemy I couldn't defeat.

All of this is in the name of creation.
All of this to leave a legacy.
All of this to have a taste in playing God.

Views

Views used to be beautiful sceneries.
Rich in history and lore.
Everyone loved and related to them.

Majestic to the eyes.
Preservation demands are high.
Technologies gave birth to cameras.

Recordings have begun.
Photos and videos have been taken.
At some point, people have also evolved.

Video recordings have become the niche.
Reviews, pranks, all various content.
Competing for what we now refer to as views.

WHs in Life

"Who are you?"
"What do you do for a living?"
"Where do you see yourself in ten years?"
"When are you getting married and having kids?"
Why are we always getting asked the above questions?

Who we are is none of their business.
What we do for a living is none of their business.
Where we see ourselves in ten years is none of their business.
When we are starting our own families is none of their business.
Why? Because it is none of their business.

You are the Alphabet

You are amazing. You are bewitching.
You are charming. You are dazzling.
You are enchanting. You are fascinating.
You are glistening. You are hardworking.
You are illuminating. You are jaw-dropping.

You are kind-hearted. You are light-hearted.
You are multi-talented. You are nimble-minded.
You are open-minded. You are pure-principled.
You are quick-witted. You are rainbow-colored.

You are scholastic. You are therapeutic.
You are unsurpassable. You are venerable.
You are welcoming. You are exhilarating.
You are youthful. You are zestful.